About the Author™

Meet
Jerry Spinelli

Alice B. McGinty

The Rosen Publishing Group's
PowerKids Press™
New York

To Jerry

Published in 2003 by The Rosen Publishing Group, Inc.
29 East 21st Street, New York, NY 10010

First Edition

Editor: Frances E. Ruffin
Book Design: Maria E. Melendez
Book Layout: Eric DePalo

Photo Credits: All photos courtesy of Jerry Spinelli and his family except p. 2 © M. Elaine Adams, courtesy of Jerry Spinelli; p. 11 Cindy Reiman; p. 15 © Melinda Hutton 1992, courtesy of Jerry Spinelli.

Grateful acknowledgment is made for permission to reprint previously published material from:
MANIAC MAGEE by Jerry Spinelli. Cover and text reprinted with permission of Little, Brown and Company.

McGinty, Alice B.
Meet Jerry Spinelli / by Alice B. McGinty.
    p. cm. — (About the author)
Includes bibliographical references and index.
Summary: Presents a brief biography of the author from Norristown, Pennsylvania, who won the Newbery Medal award in 1991 for "Maniac Magee."
ISBN 0-8239-6408-6 (library binding)
1. Spinelli, Jerry—Juvenile literature. 2. Authors, American—20th century—Biography—Juvenile literature. 3. Children's stories—Authorship—Juvenile literature. [1. Spinelli, Jerry. 2. Authors, American. 3. Authorship.] I. Title. II. Series.
PS3569.P546 Z78 2003
813'.54—dc21

2002000141

Manufactured in the United States of America

Contents

jerry spinelli

FEB- 1945

jerry spinelli

Being a Kid

Being a kid was a big job for Jerry Spinelli. There were places to explore, baseballs to hit, and yo-yo strings to untangle. When Jerry's friend came knocking at the door, shouting, "Stone war at the creek!" Jerry was ready to go. When questions popped into Jerry's head, such as "How long is eternity?" he had to have time to think about them. Jerry Spinelli didn't think about being a writer when he was a kid. He had more important things to do. However, when Jerry grew up and became a writer, all that time he had spent being a kid came in handy. It is Jerry's childhood memories and experiences that make his stories come to life.

Jerry's friends gave one another nicknames. Jerry did not like the nickname he was given, which was Spit. What Jerry did like was sports. For more than 50 years, Jerry's father was a ticket collector at the local high school's football games and a scorekeeper for its basketball games. Jerry attended many games with his dad.

◀ One of Jerry's first loves was baseball. A four-year-old Jerry is shown here in uniform.

Babar, Baseball, and Cowboy Boots

Jerry Spinelli was born on February 1, 1941, in Norristown, Pennsylvania. Along with many African American and Italian American families, Jerry's family lived in Norristown's East End. Jerry's family on his father's side was Italian. His grandfather was 14 years old when he journeyed alone from Italy to America. Jerry's father, Louis, worked as a printer. Jerry's mother, Lorna Mae Bigler, was from a **Pennsylvania Dutch** family. She enjoyed reading to Jerry and his younger brother, Bill. Jerry's favorite book was *The Story of Babar*. Jerry played baseball with his father, and he and his friends pretended they were cowboys.

An older Jerry poses in his baseball uniform. Many of the baseballs this young athlete hit went straight over the fence and into his neighbor's yard.

Early memories of the people in East End helped Jerry to bring his writing to life in his book Maniac Magee. *Jerry remembers a visit to his mother's dentist, Dr. Winters, an African American man. Jerry took a turn sitting in the patient's chair as Dr. Winters examined his mouth. Jerry remembers the dark brown color of Dr. Winters's expert fingers.*

jerry spinelli

George Street

When Jerry was six, his family moved to a house on George Street in Norristown's West End. Beyond the dead end of George Street, there were woods to explore, **salamanders** to catch, and a local zoo to visit. Jerry became friends with a group of neighborhood children. They had stone wars by the stream and threw spearlike weeds from "the spear field." They rode bikes through neighborhood alleyways and played hide-and-seek and football in the streets.

Jerry was a good student in school. He finished sixth grade as the school's spelling bee champion. Jerry was too busy playing to read a lot. However, he did like to read cereal boxes, comic books, and baseball cards.

Jerry and his younger brother, Bill, strike a cool pose in front of the family's Christmas tree.

"For the life of him, he [Maniac Magee] couldn't figure out why these East Enders called themselves black. . . . the colors he found were gingersnap and light fudge and dark fudge and acorn and butter rum and cinnamon and burnt orange. But never licorice, which to him, was real black."
—from page 51 of Maniac Magee (1990)

Sports

By the sixth grade, Jerry had become a sports nut. He won a medal for running the 50-yard (46-m) dash for the grade school track-and-field team. He played football, basketball, and little league baseball. Jerry wanted to be a shortstop for a **major league** baseball team when he grew up. Jerry continued to do well in school. In sixth grade, he wrote a poem about Mexico. It was the first poem he'd ever written. Jerry finished Stewart Junior High as class president, **prom** king, and class **valedictorian**. He was also quarterback on the school football team, guard on the basketball team, and shortstop on the baseball team.

Jerry remembers how carefully he oiled his baseball glove and placed a ball into its pocket at the end of each summer. He also remembers his baseball coach, who was famous for the "stopball" pitch, which nobody could hit. A baseball glove and the famous stopball pitch would later find their way into Jerry's book Maniac Magee.

Jerry's book Wringer *won many awards. It became a Newbery Honor Book in 1998.*

jerry spinelli

jerry spinelli

The Football Game

At Norristown High School, Jerry found life more difficult than it had been in junior high. Classes were harder. He lost the election for class president. He didn't even make it onto the varsity basketball team. One day Jerry watched his school win an exciting football game. That evening, he replayed the game in his mind. However, he wanted to do more than just think about it. So Jerry wrote a poem that captured the excitement of the game. He showed the poem to his father, who gave it to the *Times Herald*, the local newspaper. When the newspaper **published** the poem in its sports section, everyone loved it. Then Jerry knew that he would be a writer when he grew up.

◀ *This photo shows Jerry in his senior year at Norristown High School.*

"It was limp, flat, the pocket long since gone. Slowly, timidly, as though entering a shrine, the boy's fingers crept into it, flexed, curled the cracked leather, brought it back to shape, to life. He laid the new ball in the palm, pressed glove and ball together, and the glove remembered and gave way and made a pocket for the ball."
—from page 114 of *Maniac Magee* (1990)

A Young Writer

After high school, Jerry studied English at nearby Gettysburg College. He graduated in 1963. In 1964, he earned a master's degree in writing from The Johns Hopkins University in Baltimore, Maryland. Jerry worked as an **editor** for an engineering magazine. Still, he dreamed of being a writer. During his free time and lunch hours, Jerry wrote **novels** for adults. He tried to sell them to **publishers**. None were published. At work, Jerry met Eileen Mesi. One day Eileen and Jerry were waiting at a **trolley** stop. Once they were seated, Eileen dumped two notebooks of her poetry into Jerry's lap. They got to know each other better and fell in love. Jerry and Eileen were married in 1977.

Jerry and Eileen have six children and many grandchildren. Eileen Spinelli has written more than 20 books. They are mostly picture books. Their children often supply inspiration for both Jerry's and Eileen's books.

Jerry is shown receiving the Distinguished Alumni award from Gettysburg College. ▶

Chicken Bones

One morning before work, Jerry took his lunch bag from the refrigerator. He had packed some leftover fried chicken. However, when he looked into the bag, the chicken was gone. All that was left were the bones. One of his children had probably eaten his chicken. Jerry imagined **confronting** the chicken-eater. He began to write a book about what might happen. When the book was finished, Jerry sent it to publishers. The book's main character was a child, so Jerry was told to try a children's book publisher. He did, and in 1982, *Space Station Seventh Grade* was published. At 41 years old, Jerry had found his place as a writer, but he never found out who had eaten his chicken.

Jerry's first published novel, Space Station Seventh Grade, was about a 13-year-old boy. A publisher told him, "This is about a kid. Only kids will want to read it." Jerry sent the book to children's publishers and, "That's how I became a 'children's writer' by accident." Even so, Jerry doesn't believe that he writes only "for" children. "I write 'about' children. I write 'for' everybody."

17

Jerry's book Maniac Magee, which won the 1991 Newbery Medal, is about a mysterious orphan.

Success

Jerry enjoyed writing about children. The idea for his next book, *Who Put That Hair in My Toothbrush?*, which was published in 1984, came from a **rivalry** between two of his children. Jerry also thought about his own childhood on George Street, and the people he knew there. He had felt bad when an African American friend had been turned away from the public pool because of his skin color. These feelings about **prejudice** led Jerry to write the book *Maniac Magee*, published in 1990. Jerry and Eileen were awakened by a late-night phone call one year later. The caller told Jerry that *Maniac Magee* had just won the 1991 Newbery Medal, the most important award for children's **literature**.

Jerry had an African American friend who was an orphan and who ran wherever he went. *Maniac Magee* is about a white orphan, nicknamed Maniac, who ran too. Maniac finds a home with a loving African American family in the East End of town. Because of other people's prejudice, Maniac cannot stay with the family. The book is about Maniac's struggles to find a home and to understand and conquer prejudice.

Jerry often travels to different cities and signs his books for young readers who come to see him. ▶

jerry spinelli

jerry spinelli

These Days

Jerry and Eileen Spinelli live in a book-filled home in Willistown, Pennsylvania. Jerry's office is on the second floor. Eileen, who writes children's poetry, has an office down the hall. They read each other's work and suggest improvements. Jerry has published more than 21 books for children. His stories come alive with childhood memories. Nearly all of his young readers find his books realistic and honest. When he is not writing, Jerry enjoys letters from readers, playing tennis, listening to country music, and spending time with his children and grandchildren.

Jerry writes to share his experiences, feelings, thoughts, and dreams. He gives this advice to young writers. "Write what you really care about. In that way, your writing may touch the reader."

◀ *Jerry and Eileen Spinelli are shown on vacation with their children and grandchildren.*

In His Own Words

Jerry Spinelli draws on many childhood memories for his books.

What life experiences do you draw on in your writing?
Many people assume that because Eileen and I have six kids and a boatload of grandkids, that's where I get my material. Actually my primary source is probably my own memories. There is something of me and my years [living] in the West End of Norristown, Pennsylvania, in nearly every one of my books.

What's a typical working day like for you?
I write from 10:00 A.M. till noon every day that I can. When possible I also write for an hour or two at night. When you stick to it every day, it's amazing how the pages pile up.

What's your favorite thing about your job?
Hearing someone tell me that a book of mine not only gave them pleasure but that it enriched their life in some way.

What qualities do you feel have led to your success as a writer?
That might be easier for a reader to answer. I try not to be boring. I try to tell a good story and not to let the message overwhelm the story. When my characters speak in my book, I hope my readers hear something of themselves.

Are there other writers that you admire and have any of them helped you as a writer?
Absolutely . . . Eileen Spinelli. She's the one [person] a manuscript has to satisfy before it leaves the house.

Glossary

confronting (kun-FRUNT-ing) Standing up to and disagreeing with someone.

editor (EH-dih-ter) The person who corrects errors, checks facts, and decides what will be printed in a newspaper, book, or magazine.

literature (LIH-tuh-ruh-chur) Important writings that include novels, plays, and poetry.

major league (MAY-jur LEEG) A group of professional baseball teams.

novels (NAH-vulz) Long stories about imaginary people and events.

Pennsylvania Dutch (pen-sul-VAYN-yuh DUCH) People who came from Germany in the 1700s and settled in Pennsylvania for religious freedom.

prejudice (PREH-juh-dis) Disliking a group of people because they are different from you.

prom (PROM) A high school dance.

published (PUH-blishd) When something, such as a book, story, or poem, has been printed so that people can read it.

publishers (PUH-blih-shurz) People or companies whose business is printing and selling books, newspapers, or magazines.

rivalry (RY-vul-ree) When someone tries to beat someone else at something.

salamanders (SA-luh-man-durz) Animals that resemble lizards but that breathe through gills when young and don't have scaly skin.

trolley (TRAH-lee) A streetcar.

valedictorian (va-luh-dik-TOR-ee-un) The student with the highest grades, and who usually gives a speech at graduation.

Index

Web Sites

Due to the changing nature of Internet links, PowerKids Press has developed an online list of Web sites related to the subject of this book. This site is updated regularly. Please use this link to access the list:

www.powerkidslinks.com/aa/jerspin/